THE ESSENTIAL SOUP MAKER RECIPE BOOK

Fast and Delicious Meals for Every Day incl. 28 Days Meal Plan

SARAH K. PARKER

ISBN- 9798552314812

TABLE OF CONTENTS

Introduction

If you are looking to create a quick and healthy meal a soup maker is just the thing, and better still it requires minimal effort on your behalf.

Soup makers are not considered as an essential kitchen gadget however they should be. Not only can they save you time, but they also save you having a mountain of washing up to deal with! When it comes to soup recipes, they require various elements to be done such as chopping, simmering, and blending if you want a smooth consistency for your soup. Although you will have a beautiful, tasty dish you will also have a pile of washing up, mess to clear up and think what you could have been doing with the time it has taken. This process can be dealt with quickly and efficiently by a soup maker.

If you decide to use a hand-blender rather than a blender to get the right consistency for your soup you cannot achieve the ultra-smooth soup that a soup maker can provide. Better still, there are other uses for a soup maker, apart from the obvious soup, you can prepare sauces, baby food, dips, batters, smoothies and cold drinks therefore your initial investment can provide you with a multitude of different things and you can be pleased as your investment will assist you in many ways.

Two styles of Soup Maker

There are two categories that soup makers can fall into from the basic and simple, to the more sophisticated that require more input.

The simple model will see you having to chop your ingredients before pressing a button and the main use is to create soups and smoothies and will see you saving time and having to use minimal effort.

The more sophisticated soup maker is primarily a blender with several functions and whilst this device will still save you time and washing up they do require more input and if you are a less enthusiastic or beginner when it comes to cooking may prefer to use the more simple model.

Factors to consider

When it comes to purchasing a soup maker there are other factors that you may want to consider such as weight, appearance, and size. The basic models take up less space and are normally lighter whereas the more versatile soup maker models are larger and a lot heavier particularly if they have a glass jug.

You will also need to consider whether you purchase a model that has either a glass, plastic, or stainless jug. The benefit you have when using a plastic or glass jug is that you can see how your cooking is progressing whereas the stainless-steel jug does not give you this option. I would suggest that you look for a model with a timer even if it is basic a this is another good indication to check on the cooking process.

Soup Maker – Do I really want and need one?

Imagine coming home from work on a cold, dark winters night and being welcomed with a steaming hot and nutritious soup. It Is true that you could make your soup using a saucepan and your stove but do you really think you would want to go down this route if you are cold, tired and hungry? Read on to find out the advantages and disadvantages of owning a soup maker.

Advantages

- ✓ You have time that you would have spent cooking to get on with something else
- ✓ It is so easy to use, it tells you when the soup is ready and keeps it hot for some time
- ✓ You can avoid waste by using whatever you have left in your vegetable rack with a stock cube and water, twenty minutes later you have a hot, nutritious meal
- ✓ You can make excess soup and freeze, so you always have a quick go to meal
- ✓ You can get creative and make your own signature soup
- ✓ There is little to clear up, just give the soup maker a quick rinse and it is ready to use next time
- ✓ Soup makers can be used to create smoothies, drinks, dips, sauces, batter, baby food and of course soup!
- ✓ As you are in charge of what you put into your soup, you can ensure you are eating healthily, and this is a great aid for weight loss

Disadvantages

- ✓ Some may feel that the soup maker breaks with tradition whereas a child they had watched their granny making a tasty soup from not a lot and due to this they always choose to do soup making this way
- ✓ You need space and it is an extra kitchen gadget, some people feel all they need is a knife, a blender, and your stove
- ✓ There will always be some people that believe a soup maker is a luxury that they do not need
- ✓ Making soup in a soup maker can leave some people feel that they have not achieved the satisfaction that they get from cooking their soup in a pan from scratch

At the end of the day whether you buy and use a soup maker or not is your own personal choice. I think it is safe to say that there are some people who believe a soup maker is a waste of money and others who now could never liver without one!

Choosing the right Soup Maker for you

Your perfect Soup Maker

Once you have made the decision to purchase a soup maker, you will notice that there are many to choose from and that it is worth taking the time to find the one that is fit for you and what you are planning to use it for. All soup makers will ideally provide you with a completed bowl of soup however there are more than one way of getting there! There are soup makers that start from just £35 and those that will cost upwards of £100 and obviously there are varying degrees of quality.

There are some soup makers that can offer you various functions complete with different settings to create soup of various textures and consistencies. There are others that are basic offering a blending and boiling or offer only a minor function when it comes to textures and consistencies. There are machines that are fast and high powered whilst others may take a little longer and must work harder to cook the soup. Some soup makers have superb build quality whilst the cheaper ones can be less sturdy. When you look at reviews there are some soup makers that will have rave reviews whereas others may have a minimal following.

The reason for adding this to the book is to try and provide the various amount of information so that you can make the right choice that will work for you. Although there are many soup makers that will look the same, there is information that differentiates them from each other and if you know what is on offer you should be able to make the right choice for you.

The different features to consider when buying your Soup Maker

There are people who will purchase a soup maker purely by price and it is easy to think that all soup makers do the same thing and the most expensive must be the best. However, if this were the case then there would only be a choice of a few products that would all have small price points and choosing the cheapest would be the most sensible thing to do.

Due to a soup maker being a product that does have different capabilities, variations, and quality you need to compare all the features to see what options you have available to you and your budget. I am now going to go through the features in more depth, but if you are short of time and just want the basic points the key features you should be aiming for are:

Design – will this suit the décor of your kitchen and do you like the way it looks?

Size – how big is the soup maker, do you have room for it, and does it weigh much?

Speed – how quickly can it make your soup?

Power – can the soup maker chop larger vegetables, or do you need to chop everything small before cooking it?

Texture Choices – How many options do you have with regards to the consistency of your soup

Cleaning: Can you wash the soup maker in the dishwasher, or do you need to wash it by hand?

Ease of use – Is it complicated or easy for you to assemble and use?

Simplicity - Is it easy to assemble and operate, or is it a complicated appliance?

Cost – Is it affordable and what does it cost?

Soup Maker Features

The fundamental reason and aim of a soup maker is for you to save time as well as cook healthy meals, therefore if you find a soup maker that you find easy to use and that cooks your meals super quick you would be a fool not to have one.

Most soup makers that are available work quickly, however this is dependent on the features and functions that they can offer. Many may appear to be quick, but they are not going to sauté your potatoes or do other things, therefore if they seem quicker you could find that you have to do a whole lot more preparation before you can begin to cook. You will find soup makers that can do everything as in the preparation and cooking cycle, but these will be more expensive.

The gap between soup makers with regards to speed is not as big as you may think and very soup maker should be able to produce a batch of soup in under half an hour, although a faster soup maker will end up saving you time in the long run as you will not be having to do all the additional preparation that the machine can do.

Does design really matter?

There are some people that put style as their top priority and will therefore be looking for a machine that fits in with their kitchen and décor. There are soup makers that are beautiful colours, good looking, look expensive and, on the other end of the scale there are ones that you could easily mistake for a standard blender. However, this is not always defined by the price. You will see that soup makers do vary, and therefore it is so important for you to look at all the options and find the one that suits you and your kitchen best. If you find that function is more important to you over style, you can forget about this and focus on other things in your search.

So, if you are not bothered about the appearance of your soup maker looks like you may want to consider the quality of the design. The various models of soup maker that are on offer are created from various materials and some will be more rugged than others and the jug body can be made from plastic or glass. The base of the appliance could be stainless steel or something altogether different so this needs to be a consideration in your decision. Regardless of what the soup maker looks like, a better quality of build could see you purchase an appliance that is more reliable and will last you a lot longer.

Enough power to handle your recipes

You know that when you create your soup you want a soup maker that can handle everything that you chuck into it. The various soup makers that are on the market all offer their own features when it comes to the power. Some will have far more durable and stronger blades, and there are some that are slightly weaker. There are models of soup makers that have far more powerful motors that others therefore this is something else to check before you make a purchase.

How soup makers deal with ingredients is something else to consider as there are some that will find it difficult to blend large pieces of food and take far longer to do it. So, if you are looking to create thick, chunky soups the time element may not be an issue, but if you want a smoother soup occasionally then you need a soup maker that can handle everything you want to throw at it.

What size do you need?

It makes sense that you would think the larger the soup maker the more power it will have, but this may or may not be true. This is all fair however there are some that struggle with heavy kitchen equipment, particularly if it is not that easy to take apart and clean. Another consideration is that if you only have a small kitchen, a larger soup maker may take up too much valuable space that you may or may not be prepared to lose.

The advantage of choosing a larger soup maker is that it has a bigger capacity. It is crucial to go with the larger capacity if you are wanting to create big batches of soup so you can freeze some for later. You could use all your left overs, cut down on waste and make plenty of you have a big family. Most soup makers that are available to purchase have the capacity to create four large bowls of soup at any one time, but there are other which are even bigger and idea if you want to create really large portions.

Soups Consistency

When it comes to choosing the right soup maker for you, you will want to choose a model that gives you many options as this will make it far easier for you when you are making your soup. The most basic of soup makers tend to only offer two functions, this being either chunky or smooth. If you are should have a good range of options to choose from when you go to make your soup. The most basic products on the market tend to offer two option, smooth or chunky. If you are intending to be more creative with your soups it would be best for you to find a soup maker that provides you with more choices.

There are soup makers for sale that allow you to control the soup making process whilst it is cooking. The additional features may include a pulse button, additional buttons that let you mix the soup and if you find that you are not happy with the soup you are making you can even alter the soup mid-way through the cooking process. It may be that you feel you need more power, and if this is the case my advice would be to look for the soup maker that offers you the extra functions and features. However, if you are happy to just switch your soup maker on, press the button and let it do the job, then you should find that a basic model will be right for you.

Cleaning

When you are out shopping the last thing, you will be thinking about is how easy it will be to clean the soup maker, however, it is a crucial factor and one you should heed. The main issue with soup makers is that they are awkward to clean. There are a lot of soup makers that are difficult to take apart, some that are not suitable for the dishwasher and believe me certain soup makers can be an absolute nightmare to clean.

There are alternative soup makers that offer a self-clean function, and all you must do is add some washing up liquid in the jug and then turn on the cleaning option. This is an excellent feature and one that I would suggest you look out for. There are soup makers that do not have this option, and if this is the model you choose it is imperative that you rinse out the soup maker straight after using it, it should be left to soak so that there is no food stuck. Most importantly though, take care that you do not catch the blade and cut yourself.

There are soup makers that have cleaning tools included and if you choose a model that does not offer self-cleaning this is a great extra that will make cleaning your soup maker a whole lot easier.

Do the simple things really matter?

There is no doubt that when you purchase any kitchen appliance it is always better to choose one that is simple to use. Quite often if the instructions are confusing, the appliance is complicated, or it is difficult to assemble it can be very frustrating and many just give up and the appliance then sits in the corner collecting dust. Buying a soup maker should result in you having fun and getting creative with the appliance. Therefore, a soup maker should be easy to use, clean and generally a productive appliance for your kitchen.

Most soup makers are easy to use particularly the more basic and inexpensive models. Generally, you can fill with your chosen liquid and ingredients and the soup maker is then ready to cook.

With the increase in function and more options come more choices and there is a chance that you may encounter some confusion. When it comes to a good soup maker, it should provide clear and easy to follow instructions but above all be easy for you to operate. When you take the soup maker out of the box it should be easy for you to assemble and as far as the cooking goes even if you have little experience with kitchen appliances it should be easy for you to work out.

If you do not want the hassle of a soup maker that needs a lot of assembly and management or one that you have to stand over and watch cook because you have to flick certain buttons on at different stages of cooking you may want to go with a more basic appliance. However, it is important to shop around as there are the middle of the range soup makers that offer some features and functions and are relatively easy to assemble and work. Do not be fooled into thinking that you need the extremely basic model unless it is purely something that you want to use every now and again.

Another reason to opt for a slightly more hi-tech soup maker is that you can make so much more with a soup maker than just soup, you can create smoothies, desserts and pasta dished to name but a few.

What will it cost?

Unfortunately, for many of us cost is a major factor when we decide to purchase any type of luxury items, and this cannot be ignored. Even if you do not realise the cost of a soup maker will factor into your decision. There are some excellent value soup makers on the market and due to the breadth of the range there should be a soup maker that falls into most people's budget. Obviously, there are more expensive models which have a stronger build and offer various features and functions, and the more expensive models do usually come with an extensive guarantee period which is ideal if you come across any problems with the soup maker.

Do not fall into the thought process that the more expensive the product is the better it will perform because this is not necessarily true. The only piece of advice I can offer you is to check the reviews that you can find online and you can also compare models this way. Take your time and do your own research so that when you purchase your soup maker you know that you are making the right choice for you and what you want to do. If you fall into the trap of letting price guide your decision you could end up disappointed with the purchase that you make.

Tips & Handy Hints with your Soup Maker

I have created the following hints and tips do that you can make the most of your soup maker, some may be common sense but hopefully there will be a little something that helps you out.

1) Prepare your ingredients in advance, most recipes are just chop and drop and by having the ingredients ready you will have more time for other things

2) When it comes to liquid or stock use boiling water. I have found that if I use tap water the vegetables sometime are not fully cooked, another plus for hot stock is it adds even more flavour to the finished product

3) Thaw any frozen ingredients fully before using

4) Any meat you use for your recipes should be pre-cooked as there is not enough settings to ensure the meat gets cooked through

5) Potatoes, turnips, and carrots need to be chopped into small pieces as this will give them time to cook thoroughly in the short space of time it takes to make your soup

6) Whenever you use your soup maker be sure that the lid is closed properly.

7) Do not take the lid off during the cooking process unless it is a model that you can as you could end up getting burnt by the boiling hot liquid

8) Follow the manufacturer's instructions and adhere to them as this will ensure that there are no mishaps, such as overfilling the appliance

9) Never put the soup maker fully submerged into water when it comes to cleaning. It is vital that you again follow the instructions to the letter, or you could end up breaking the machine or worse getting an electric shock

10) The most important thing to remember is have fun! Use your soup maker to its full advantage and you can enjoy hot soups and cool smoothies for years to come

Breakfast

Berry Mixed Smoothie

Time: 10 minutes / Serving 1
Net Carbs: 16g / 0.56oz Fat: 4g / 0.14oz
Protein: 3g / 0.10oz Kcal: 98

Ingredients:

- 450ml / 2 cups of unsweetened almond milk
- 450ml / 2 cups of frozen fruit
- 32g / ¼ cup of spinach
- 2 tablespoons of erythritol

Instructions:

1. Add all do the ingredients to your soup maker and use the blend option

2. Blend for 2 minutes until thick and smooth

3. Serve and enjoy

Incredible Immune Boosting Smoothie

Time: 3 minutes / Serving 1
Net Carbs: 31g / 1.09oz Fat: 4g / 0.14oz
Protein: 3g / 0.10oz Kcal: 156

Ingredients:

- 250ml / 8fl oz almond milk
- 1 Weetabix
- 1 banana
- 2 raw broccoli florets
- 2 strawberries
- 150ml / 5fl oz of water

Instructions:

1. Place everything into your soup maker and blend until smooth
2. Serve and enjoy

Super Breakfast Shake

Time: 5 minutes / Serving 1
Net Carbs: 50g / 1.76oz Fat: 12g / 0.42oz
Protein: 15g / 0.53oz Kcal: 391

Ingredients:

- 100ml milk / half a cup (full fat)
- 2 tablespoons of natural yoghurt
- 1 banana
- 150g / 2/3 of a cup of frozen berries
- 50g / 1/3 of a cup of fresh blueberries
- 1 tablespoon of chia seeds
- 1 tablespoon of goji berries
- 1 tablespoon of seeds (mixed)
- 1 tablespoon of honey
- ½ teaspoon of cinnamon

Instructions:

1. Place everything into your soup maker and blend until smooth
2. Enjoy

Two Minute Breakfast Shake

Time: 2 minutes / Serving 2
Net Carbs: 25g / 0.88oz Fat: 3g / 0.10oz
Protein: 4g / 0.14oz Kcal: 156

Ingredients:

- 1 banana
- 1 tablespoon of porridge oats
- 80g / 2.8oz of soft fruits

- 150ml / 5fl oz of milk
- 1 teaspoon of honey
- 1 teaspoon of vanilla extract

Instructions:

1. Place everything into your soup maker and blend until smooth

Beautiful Banana Smoothie

Time: 5 minutes / Serving 2
Net Carbs: 29g / 1.02oz Fat: 11g / 0.39oz
Protein: 5g / 0.18oz Kcal: 250

Ingredients:

- 500ml / 16.9oz almond milk (unsweetened)
- 6 prunes
- 1 small, ripened banana
- 1 teaspoon of cinnamon

Instructions:

1. Place everything into your soup maker and blend until smooth
2. Chill and then serve

Super Strawberry & Green Smoothie

Time: 5 minutes / Serving 2
Net Carbs: 16g / 0.56oz Fat: 13g / 0.46oz
Protein: 8g / 0.28oz Kcal: 226

Ingredients:

- 160g / 5.6oz ripe strawberries
- 160g / 5.6oz of baby spinach
- 1 small, halved avocado with the flesh scooped out
- 150ml / 5fl oz bio yoghurt
- Juice from 2 small oranges
- ½ teaspoon of finely grated orange zest

Instructions:

1. Place everything into your soup maker and blend until smooth

Remarkable Raspberry & Awesome Apple Smoothie

Time: 5 minutes / Serving 4
Net Carbs: 14g / 0.49oz Fat: 3g / 0.10oz
Protein: 4g / 0.14oz Kcal: 106

Ingredients:

- 2 cored apples
- 150g / 1/3 of a cup of frozen raspberries
- 150ml / 5fl oz natural yoghurt
- 100ml / 3.3fl oz milk
- 2 tablespoons / 1 oz of porridge oats
- Juice from ½ a lemon

Instructions:

1. Place everything into your soup maker and blend until smooth
2. Add 50ml of milk or water if you prefer a thinner consistency

Sensational Summertime Smoothie

Time: 5 minutes / Serving 3
Net Carbs: 30g / 1.06oz Fat: 4g / 0.14oz
Protein: 3g / 0.10oz Kcal: 171

Ingredients:

- 🍽 500ml / 16.9oz chilled carrot juice
- 🍽 200g / 7.1oz tinned or fresh pineapple
- 🍽 2 bananas thickly sliced
- 🍽 20g / 0.71 cashew nuts
- 🍽 Small piece of peeled ginger
- 🍽 Juice of a lime

Instructions:

1. Place everything into your soup maker and blend until smooth
2. Drink straight away or take it with you for later

Curly Kale Smoothie

Time: 5 minutes / Serving 2
Net Carbs: 8g / 0.28oz Fat: 11g / 0.39oz
Protein: 4g / 0.14oz Kcal: 127

Ingredients:

- ½ avocado
- 2 handfuls of kale
- Juice from ½ lime
- 1 banana
- Handful of frozen pineapple chunks
- Medium chunk of ginger
- 1 tablespoon cashew nuts

Instructions:

1. Add everything to your soup maker and blend until smooth
2. Add more water if you prefer a thinner drink

Cheerful Cherry Smoothie

Time: 10 minutes / Serving 2-4
Net Carbs: 16g / 0.56oz Fat: 1g / 0.03oz
Protein: 3g / 0.10oz Kcal: 90

Ingredients:

- 300g / 10.6oz of pitted cherries
- 150g / 1/3 of a cup of / 2/3 of a cup of natural yoghurt
- 1 large slice banana
- ½ teaspoon of vanilla extract

Instructions:

1. Add everything to your soup maker and blend until smooth
2. Add more water if you prefer a thinner drink
3. Stir thoroughly and pour into 4 glasses

Lunch

Lentil Soup

Time: 35 minutes / Serving 4
Net Carbs: 15g / 0.53oz Fat: 1g / 0.03oz
Protein: 6g / 0.21oz Kcal: 103

Ingredients:

- 75g / 2.65oz of red lentils
- 750ml / 25.3oz ham or vegetable stock
- 3 finely chopped carrots
- 1 sliced medium leek
- Handful of chopped parsley

Instructions:

1. Add the lentils, carrots, leek, and stock
2. Choose the 'chunky soup' function on your soup maker
3. The soup will foam at the start, but this will disappear when cooked
4. When complete check the lentils are well and season
5. Scatter with parsley, serve and enjoy

50 Calorie Green Goodness Soup

Time: 35 minutes / Serving 4
Net Carbs: 11g / 0.39oz Fat: 2g / 0.07oz
Protein: 23g / 0.81oz Kcal: 50

Ingredients:

- 1 peeled and finely diced onion
- 600ml / 20.3oz vegetable stock
- 500g / 17.6oz assorted salad leaves
- 4 trimmed and chopped spring onions
- 2 tablespoons / 1 oz of chopped mint
- 2 teaspoons of cornflour mixed with a little milk
- 200ml / 6.8oz skimmed milk
- Salt and pepper to season

Instructions:

1. Put the stock, and onions into the soup maker and simmer for 10 minutes
2. Add the salad leaves, replace the lid and simmer for another 20 minutes
3. Add the mint and cook for a further 2 minutes
4. Choose the smooth soup function
5. Add the cornflour mix to the milk and add to the soup
6. Cook for a further 5 minutes on the smooth soup
7. Stir, season with salt and pepper
8. Serve and enjoy

Marvellous Mushroom Soup

Time: 35 minutes / Serving 4
Net Carbs: 6g / 0.21oz Fat: 4g / 0.14oz
Protein: 9g / 0.32oz Kcal: 94

Ingredients:

- 2 roughly chopped medium onions
- 1 crushed garlic clove
- 500g / 17.6oz well chopped mushrooms
- 750ml / 25.4oz chicken stock
- 4 tbsp single cream
- Handful roughly chopped parsley

Instructions:

1. Add the mushrooms, onions, garlic, and chicken stock to soup maker, choose the smooth soup setting, check that you have not overfilled the soup maker

2. When the soup maker has completed its program, stir the soup, and add the cream

3. Blitz the soup until creamy

4. Serve topped with parsley an additional cream if desired

Colourful Coriander & Carrot Soup

Time: 30 minutes / Serving 2
Net Carbs: 14g / 0.49oz Fat: 2g / 0.07oz
Protein: 9g / 0.32oz Kcal: 133

Ingredients:

- 1 chopped small onion
- 1 small peeled and chopped potato
- 400g / 14.1oz peeled and chopped carrots
- 600ml / 20.2oz of chicken or vegetable stock
- ½ bunch of coriander

Instructions:

1. Put all your ingredients except the coriander into the soup maker and select the smooth soup program
2. Once complete, season the soup and add the coriander
3. Blend again until completely combined
4. Serve and enjoy

Tasty Tomato Soup

Time: 35 minutes / Serving 2
Net Carbs: 14g / 0.49oz Fat: 1g / 0.03oz
Protein: 3g / 0.10oz Kcal: 85

Ingredients:

- 1 chopped small onion
- ½ small peeled, chopped carrot
- ½ stick of chopped celery
- 500g / 17.6oz halved or quartered ripe tomatoes

- 450ml / 2 cups of vegetable stock
- 1 teaspoon of tomato puree
- Pinch of salt

Instructions:

1. Put all your ingredients into the soup maker and select the smooth soup program

2. When complete season well and taste

3. Add more tomato puree to give the soup a richer colour, sugar, or salt if desired

Banging Butternut Squash Soup

Time: 1 hour 10 minutes / Serving 2
Net Carbs: 28g / 0.99oz Fat: 15g / 0.53oz
Protein: 5g / 0.18oz Kcal: 272

Ingredients:

- 500g / 17.6oz peeled and cubed butternut squash
- 1 diced onion
- 1 thinly sliced garlic clove
- 1 mild, deseeded, and thinly chopped red chili
- 2 tablespoons / 1 oz of crème fraise
- ½ tablespoon of olive oil

Instructions:

1. Heat your oven to 200C
2. Put the butternut squash in a roasting pan, add the olive oil and roast for half an hour until soft and golden
3. Add the roasted squash to your soup maker and select the smooth soup function
4. Add the garlic, onion most of the chili and the stock
5. Season well and start the soup maker
6. Once the cycle completes, season your soup well before adding the crème fraiche
7. Blend again and add some boiling water to get your favoured consistency
8. Serve in bowls topped with crème fraiche and chopped chili, enjoy

Luscious Leek & Potato Soup

Time: 35 minutes / Serving 2
Net Carbs: 24g / 0.85oz Fat: 16g / 0.56oz
Protein: 12g / 0.42oz Kcal: 300

Ingredients:

- 1 small onion cubed
- 1 sliced large leek
- 225g / 7.9oz peeled potatoes cut into the same size as cubed onion
- 450ml / 2 cups of vegetable stock
- 60ml / 2oz whole milk
- 60ml / 2oz whipping cream
- 1 small knob of butter
- Chives finely chopped

Instructions:

1. Add the potatoes, onions, all bar one handful of the leeks and the stock to your soup maker

2. Choose the smooth soup function

3. Once completed add most of the milk and cream then blend again

4. Turn on the 'keep warm' / 'heat' to keep the soup warm

5. Shred the rest of the white part of the leek, heat the butter and gently fry the leek for a few minutes until it is soft but not coloured

6. Swirl the remaining cream onto your soup and top with the remaining leeks, black pepper and chives

Soup Maker Portuguese Fish Soup

Time: 30 minutes / Serving 4
Net Carbs: 19g / 0.67oz Fat: 1g / 0.03oz
Protein: 14g / 0.49oz Kcal: 190

Ingredients:

- 1 carrot
- 2 potatoes
- 1 red pepper
- 100g / 3.5oz white fish
- 100g / 3.5oz of clams
- 100g / 3.5oz of prawns
- 1 tin of tomatoes
- 1/3 glass of red wine
- 2 teaspoons of garlic puree
- 1 teaspoon of mustard
- 2 teaspoons of paprika
- 100ml / 3.4oz of water
- Salt and pepper

Instructions:

1. Peel the carrots and potatoes then chop
2. Dice the red pepper and white fish
3. Add them all to the soup maker
4. Add the uncooked seafood
5. Add the wine, tomatoes, and seasoning
6. Mix well and select the chunky soup function
7. Cook for 25 minutes, serve, and enjoy

Majestic Mediterranean Veggie Soup

Time: 35 minutes / Serving 4
Net Carbs: 33g / 1.16oz Fat: 3g / 0.10oz
Protein: 4g / 0.14oz Kcal: 169

Ingredients:

- 50ml / 1.7oz of water
- 1 small red pepper
- 2 large onions
- 100g / 3.5oz green beans
- 5 carrots
- 1 leek
- 1 peeled sweet potato
- 1 peeled potato
- 1 tin of tomatoes
- 1 tablespoon of oregano
- 1 teaspoon of chives
- 1 teaspoon of thyme
- 2 teaspoons of pureed garlic
- 2 tablespoons of garlic & herb soft cheese
- Salt and pepper

Instructions:

1. Chop up the vegetables and add to bottom of your soup maker
2. Add tinned tomatoes
3. Add the seasoning and water
4. Cook using the basic soup feature for 30 minutes for a tasty chunky soup

Super, Speedy Soup

Time: 30 minutes / Serving 4
Net Carbs: 26g / 0.92oz Fat: 1g / 0.03oz
Protein: 3g / 0.10oz. Kcal: 111

Ingredients:

- 3 tomatoes
- 1 onion
- 6 carrots
- 2 mixed peppers
- 1 leek
- 150g / 5.3oz of peeled and cubed butternut squash
- 2 tins of tomatoes
- 1 teaspoon of pureed garlic
- ½ teaspoon of powdered chili
- ½ teaspoon of cayenne pepper
- Salt and pepper if required
- 200ml / 6.8oz of water

Instructions:

1. Wash and slice the leek

2. Peel the carrots and onion

3. Deseed the peppers

4. Chop the tomatoes, carrots, onion, and mixed peppers

5. Put all ingredients into the soup maker season and add the 200ml of water

6. Set the timer for 28 minutes on the chunky soup setting

7. Add the tinned tomatoes and blend until smooth

8. Serve and enjoy

Vegetable Thai Soup Maker Curry

Time: 30 minutes / Serving 4
Net Carbs: 21g / 0.74oz Fat: 24g / 0.85oz
Protein: 4g / 0.14oz Kcal: 302

Ingredients:

- 1 leek
- 3 carrots
- 1 courgette
- 200g / 7.1oz peeled, diced pumpkin
- 1 red pepper
- 1 tin of coconut milk
- 1 teaspoon of Thai Curry paste
- 1 teaspoon garlic puree
- 1 teaspoon of mustard
- 1 teaspoon of coriander
- 2 teaspoons of paprika
- 1 teaspoon of mixed spice
- 100ml / 3.4oz of water
- Salt and pepper

Instructions:

1. Peel the carrots and dice the red pepper, leek, courgette, and carrots
2. Put all the vegetables into your soup maker, add the coconut milk and water
3. Sprinkle the seasoning across the top
4. Choose the chunky soup setting and cook for 25 minutes
5. Serve and enjoy

Parsnip Perfection Soup

Time: 30 minutes / Serving 4
Net Carbs: 46g / 1.62oz Fat: 0g / 0.00oz
Protein: 3g / 0.10oz Kcal: 197

Ingredients:

- 2 sweet potatoes
- 1 onion
- 4 parsnips
- 2 carrots

- 1 teaspoon of pureed garlic
- 1 teaspoon of thyme
- Salt and pepper
- 100ml / 3.4oz water

Instructions:

1. Peel chop the sweet potatoes, parsnips, carrots, and onion and put them into your soup maker

2. Add the pureed garlic, water, and season

3. Cook for 25 minutes using the blend feature

4. Serve and enjoy

Souper Salad Soup

Time: 30 minutes / Serving 4
Net Carbs: 16g / 0.56oz Fat: 0g / 0.00oz
Protein: 2g / 0.07oz Kcal: 75

Ingredients:

- ¼ of a white cabbage
- 1 green pepper
- 1 red pepper
- 4 carrots
- 3 sticks of celery
- 2 tomatoes
- 1 teaspoon of oregano
- 100ml / 3.4oz of water
- Salt and pepper

Instructions:

1. Peel the carrots, deseed the peppers and chop all the salad ingredients
2. Put everything into your soup maker with the seasoning and water
3. Cooked for 25 minutes using the blend feature
4. Serve and enjoy

Clearly Skinny Celery Soup

Time: 30 minutes / Serving 4
Net Carbs: 10g / 0.35oz Fat: 3g / 0.10oz
Protein: 4g / 0.14oz Kcal: 76

Ingredients:

- 6 sticks of celery
- 1 peeled onion
- 4 peeled carrots
- 250ml / 8.5oz water

- 2 tablespoons of cream cheese
- 1 teaspoon of chives
- 1 teaspoon of mixed herbs
- Salt and pepper

Instructions:

1. Chop the celery into pieces of 1cm and put into your soup maker
2. Dice the carrots and onion and add to the soup maker
3. Add the seasoning and water then cook on the blend function for 25 minutes
4. Add the cream cheese to thicken, blend and serve

Blended Broccoli Soup

Time: 30 minutes / Serving 4
Net Carbs: 13g / 0.46oz Fat: 0g / 0.00oz
Protein: 5g / 0.18oz. Kcal: 70

Ingredients:

- ½ courgette
- 1 small, peeled onion
- 1 teaspoon of thyme
- 2 tablespoons of Greek yoghurt
- 1 medium head of broccoli
- 1 teaspoon of oregano
- 468ml / 15.8oz water
- Salt and pepper

Instructions:

1. Chop up the courgette and broccoli and add to soup maker
2. Add the water and season
3. Cook using the blend function for 25 minutes
4. Add the Greek yoghurt and stir thoroughly
5. Serve and enjoy

Potato Sweet Soup

Time: 30 minutes / Serving 4
Net Carbs: 45g / 1.59oz Fat: 2g / 0.07oz
Protein: 6g / 0.21oz. Kcal: 217

Ingredients:

- 800g / 28.2oz of sweet potatoes diced
- 1 tablespoon of paprika
- Salt and pepper to season
- 200ml / 6.8oz of milk
- 2 tablespoons of coriander
- 500ml / 16.9oz of water

Instructions:

1. Put the diced sweet potato into the soup maker
2. Add the seasoning and 300ml water
3. Cook for 25 minutes using the chunky soup setting
4. Add the milk and an additional 200ml of water and blend until smooth

Utterly, Buttery Butternut Squash Soup

Time: 35 minutes / Serving 2
Net Carbs: 47g / 1.66oz Fat: 1g / 0.03oz
Protein: 5g / 0.18oz. Kcal: 190

Ingredients:

- 750g / 26.4oz butternut squash
- 200ml / 6.8oz vegetable stock
- 2 teaspoons of coriander
- 2 teaspoons of cumin
- 1 teaspoon of tandoori seasoning
- ½ teaspoon of mixed spice
- Salt and pepper

Instructions:

1. Slice and peel the butternut squash, remove all the seeds
2. Place all the ingredients except the butternut squash into your soup maker and mix
3. Add as much butternut squash as you can to the soup maker
4. Cook on the chunky soup setting
5. Stir and check you have enough liquid and blend
6. Pour into bowls, serve, and enjoy

Cocktail of Prawn Soup

Time: 30 minutes / Serving 2
Net Carbs: 26g / 0.92oz Fat: 3g / 0.10oz
Protein: 7g / 0.25oz. Kcal: 172

Ingredients:

- 1 bag of king prawns (fresh)
- 1 peeled and diced onion
- 1 tablespoon of pureed garlic
- 1 teaspoon of powdered chili
- 1 teaspoon of basil
- Salt and pepper if required
- 250ml / 8.5oz of tomato sauce
- 1 red pepper deseeded
- 1 tablespoon of peeled and grated ginger
- 1 teaspoon of mixed spice
- 1 teaspoon of coriander

Instructions:

1. Add the ingredients to your soup maker and steam for 25 minutes
2. Once cooked, use the blend setting
3. Serve and enjoy

Complete Cauliflower Soup

Time: 30 minutes / Serving 6
Net Carbs: 19g / 0.67oz Fat: 0g / 0.00oz
Protein: 3g / 0.10oz. Kcal: 85

Ingredients:

- 1 medium cauliflower
- 1 peeled and seedless butternut squash
- 4 tablespoons of Greek yoghurt
- 1 teaspoon of parsley

- Salt and pepper
- 1 peeled large onion
- 1 yellow pepper
- 250ml / 8.5oz water
- 1 teaspoon of mixed herbs

Instructions:

1. Chop the cauliflower into small florets and add to your soup maker
2. Chop the pepper and remove the seeds then add to your soup maker
3. Chop the butternut squash and onions and add to soup maker
4. Add the water and season
5. Cook for 25 minutes using the cook and blend function
6. Add the Greek yoghurt once cooked and stir thoroughly
7. Serve and enjoy

Dinner

Roast Dinner Soup

Time: 13 minutes / Serving 4
Net Carbs: 42g / 1.48oz Fat: 9g / 0.32oz
Protein: 10g / 0.35oz Kcal: 288

Ingredients:

- 30g / 1.1oz turkey
- 100g / 3.5oz instant cauliflower cheese
- 5 parsnips, roasted
- 25g / 0.9oz brussels sprouts
- 1 teaspoon chives
- Salt and pepper
- 2 yorkshire puddings
- 5 roast potatoes
- 2 tablespoons of mash potato
- 1 tablespoon of gravy
- 2 teaspoons of parsley
- 150ml / 5fl oz of water

Instructions:

1. Chop all ingredients and put them in the soup maker
2. Add the water
3. Add the seasoning and set the soup maker to the blend function then cook for 10 minutes
4. As the ingredients are already cooked you are just blending and heating them up
5. Serve and enjoy

Tasty Turkey Soup

Time: 24 minutes / Serving 2
Net Carbs: 56g / 1.97oz Fat: 5g / 0.18oz
Protein: 22g / 0.78oz Kcal: 353

Ingredients:

- 200ml / 6.8oz turkey stock
- 100g / 3.5oz shredded vegetables
- 2 teaspoon cumin
- Salt and pepper
- 3 white potatoes
- 150g / 5.3oz of shredded turkey
- 1 teaspoon tandoori seasoning

Instructions:

1. Add the turkey stock to the soup maker
2. Dice the potatoes and mix into the stock
3. Put the shredded vegetables on the top (as much as you can fit)
4. Put the lid on your soup maker and cook for 22 minutes
5. Add the seasoning and shredded turkey
6. Blend using the soup blend button
7. Serve and enjoy

Minestrone Homemade Soup

Time: 35 minutes / Serving 6
Net Carbs: 41g/1.45oz Fat: 0g/0.00oz
Protein: 10g/0.35oz Kcal: 217

Ingredients:

- 6 carrots
- 1 onion
- ½ bag of spinach
- 1 tin of tomatoes
- 50g / 1.8oz of frozen peas
- 2 teaspoons of tomato puree
- 150ml / 5.1oz of water
- 1 teaspoon of rosemary
- Salt and pepper

- 3 medium mushrooms
- Handful of brussels sprouts
- 3 fresh tomatoes
- 1 tin of kidney beans
- 2 teaspoons garlic puree
- 100g / 3.5oz pasta ditalini
- 1 teaspoon of oregano
- Handful of bay leaves

Instructions:

1. Peel and dice the onion and carrots, then dice the mushrooms and tomato and put in the soup maker

2. Add the spinach, Brussel sprouts, peas, pasta, kidney beans and seasoning

3. Pour the water over the ingredients and cook for 20 minutes on the chunky soup setting

4. Serve and enjoy

Sensational Stilton & Broccoli Soup

Time: 35 minutes / Serving 4
Net Carbs: 17g / 0.60oz Fat: 14g / 0.49oz
Protein: 16g / 0.56oz Kcal: 275

Ingredients:

- 1 finely chopped onion
- 1 sliced leek
- 1 sliced stick of celery
- 1 diced medium potato
- 750ml / 25.3oz vegetable stock
- 1 roughly chopped head of broccoli
- 140g / 4.9oz of crumbled stilton cheese

Instructions:

1. Put all the ingredients into your soup maker apart from the stilton
2. Choose the smooth soup program
3. Once completed, season and stir in most of the cheese
4. Blend again until the cheese is melted and well combined
5. Season with black pepper, top with remaining stilton
6. Serve and enjoy

Cheeky Chicken Soup

Time: 35 minutes / Serving 2
Net Carbs: 8g / 0.28oz Fat: 5g / 0.18oz
Protein: 17g / 0.60oz Kcal: 155

Ingredients:

- 1 chopped onion
- 1 chopped large carrot
- 700ml / 23.7oz of chicken stock
- 150g / 5.3oz of skinless, shredded roast chicken
- 100g / 3.5oz frozen peas
- 1 ½ tablespoons of Greek yoghurt
- ½ small, crushed garlic clove
- Squeeze of lemon juice

Instructions:

1. Add the carrots, onion, and peas to your soup maker
2. Choose the chunky soup program
3. Once the program ends stir in the chicken and leave to warm
4. Mix the garlic, yoghurt, and lemon juice together
5. Season and pour into bowls, add the rest of the yoghurt, and serve

Variety, Vegetable Soup

Time: 35 minutes / Serving 2
Net Carbs: 32g / 1.13oz Fat: 1g / 0.03oz
Protein: 4g / 0.14oz Kcal: 166

Ingredients:

- 🍽 200g / 7.1oz of chopped vegetables such as carrots, celery, and onions
- 🍽 300g / 10.6oz peeled and chopped potato
- 🍽 700ml / 23.7oz vegetable stock
- 🍽 Fresh herbs and crème fraiche to serve

Instructions:

1. Add the potatoes, vegetables, and stock to your soup maker

2. Choose the smooth soup program

3. When the program is complete pour into bowls top with a little crème fraiche and herbs

4. Enjoy

Perfect Pea and Ham Soup

Time: 35 minutes / Serving 4
Net Carbs: 24g / 0.85oz Fat: 6g / 0.21oz
Protein: 24g / 0.85oz Kcal: 260

Ingredients:

- 🍽 1 chopped onion

- 🍽 1 peeled and diced potato

- 🍽 1 litre of pork or ham stock

- 🍽 500g / 17.6oz frozen peas

- 🍽 300g / 10.6oz of thick sliced lean ham

- 🍽 200g / 7.1oz of chopped vegetables such as carrots, celery, and onions

Instructions:

1. Add the potatoes, onions, peas, and stock to your soup maker

2. Use the smooth soup program

3. Once completed stir in the ham, season, and serve

Cheddar Potato & Sausage Soup

Time: 40 minutes / Serving 4
Net Carbs: 19g / 0.67oz Fat: 13g / 0.46oz
Protein: 14g / 0.49oz Kcal: 294

Ingredients:

- 1 tablespoon of butter
- 250g / 1/3 of a cup of / 1 cup of potatoes
- 75g / ¾ cup of mature cheddar cheese
- 500ml / 2 ½ cups of vegetable stock
- 50ml / ¼ cup of double cream
- 2 Italian sausages with skins removed
- ½ teaspoon of thyme
- 1 teaspoon of minced garlic
- 1 teaspoon of Italian herbs
- 1 teaspoon of minced garlic
- 1 medium carrot
- 2 sticks of celery
- 1 small onion
- Salt and pepper

Instructions:

1. Cut vegetables into big chunks

2. Add the onion, butter, garlic, and herbs to your soup maker and select the 'sauté' or similar setting and cook for 5 minutes

3. Add the vegetables, cheese and stock and set to smooth on the soup maker

4. When there is 2 minutes left add in the cream

5. In a frying pan fry the sausage until crisp and golden

6. Once the soup is ready season with salt and pepper

7. Serve in bowls with the sausage sprinkled on top

Ravishing Rainbow Bowl

Time: 20 minutes / Serving 2
Net Carbs: 19g / 0.67oz Fat: 16g / 0.56oz
Protein: 4g / 0.14oz Kcal: 251

Ingredients:

- 🍽 1 stoned, peeled, and halved avocado
- 🍽 1 stoned, peeled and chunked ripe mango
- 🍽 1 cored, chunked apple
- 🍽 1 peeled and chunked dragon fruit
- 🍽 200ml almond milk
- 🍽 50g / 1/3 of a cup of spinach
- 🍽 100g mixed berries

Instructions:

1. Add the avocado, mango, spinach, apple and almond milk into your soup maker and pulse until smooth and thick
2. Serve in two bowls topped with the mixed berries and dragon fruit

Magnificent Mac n Cheese

Time: 30 minutes / Serving 4
Net Carbs: 43g / 1.52oz Fat: 33g / 1.16oz
Protein: 21g / 0.74oz Kcal: 558

Ingredients:

- ½ cauliflower
- 200g / 7.1oz cheddar cheese
- 2 teaspoons of pureed garlic
- 1 teaspoon of basil
- 1 peeled and diced small onion
- 450g / 15.8oz of macaroni
- 300ml / 10.1 oz coconut milk
- 100ml / 3.4oz of water
- 1 teaspoon of mixed herbs
- 1 teaspoon of oregano
- Salt and pepper

Instructions:

1. Put the pasta, water and cauliflower into your soup maker and cook on the chunky soup function for 20 minutes

2. Drain the water and put the pasta to the side

3. Add the onion to the cooked cauliflower with the coconut milk, garlic puree, cheese and seasoning to your soup maker and blend for three minutes

4. Add the pasta and cook in the soup maker for a further 6 minutes

5. Add some grated cheese prior to serving

Pea Minty Soup

Time: 28 minutes / Serving 4
Net Carbs: 24g / 0.85oz Fat: 3g / 0.10oz
Protein: 11g / 0.39oz. Kcal: 168

Ingredients:

- 500g / 17.6oz of frozen garden peas
- 2 tablespoons / 1/8 of a cup of Greek yoghurt
- 2 peeled onions
- 1 teaspoon of fresh mint
- 50g / 1/3 of a cup of mozzarella cheese
- 250ml / 8.5oz water
- 1 teaspoon garlic puree
- 1 tablespoon of parsley
- Salt and pepper

Instructions:

1. Dice the onion and then add all ingredients to soup maker
2. Cook for 25 minutes using the blend function
3. Add further water or yoghurt if required
4. Serve and enjoy

Moroccan Creamy Carrot Soup

Time: 40 minutes / Serving 4
Net Carbs: 34g / 1.20oz Fat: 24g / 0.85oz
Protein: 5g / 0.18oz. Kcal: 35

Ingredients:

- 12 large carrots
- 1 pepper, red
- 1 tablespoon of honey
- 100ml / 3.4oz of water
- 1 teaspoon of turmeric
- 2 tablespoons / 1/8 of a cup of coriander

- 1 onion
- 2 teaspoon pureed garlic
- 1 tin of coconut milk
- 1 teaspoon of cinnamon
- 1 grated, peeled cube of ginger
- Salt and pepper

Instructions:

1. Peel and dice the carrots and onion, and dice the pepper
2. Add to your soup maker
3. Add the rest of the ingredients
4. Cook for 25 minutes using the soup blended setting
5. Pour into bowls and enjoy

Cheesy Cauliflower Soup

Time: 30 minutes / Serving 4
Net Carbs: 13g / 0.46oz Fat: 10g / 0.35oz
Protein: 13g / 0.46oz Kcal: 197

Ingredients:

- 250g / 1/3 of a cup of cauliflower florets
- 100g / 3.5oz of cheddar cheese
- 1 teaspoon of basil
- 300ml / 10.1oz water
- 200ml / 6.8oz milk
- 100ml / 3.4oz Greek yoghurt
- Salt and pepper

Instructions:

1. Cut the cauliflower into small florets and place in the bottom of your soup maker
2. Add the water and seasoning
3. Cook using the chunky soup for 28 minutes
4. Add the milk and Greek yoghurt and blend
5. Add the cheese and mix thoroughly
6. Serve and enjoy

Greek Greens Soup

Time: 35 minutes / Serving 2
Net Carbs: 11g / 0.38oz Fat: 0g / 0.00oz
Protein: 4g / 0.14oz. Kcal: 58

Ingredients:

- ½ courgette
- 100g / 3.5oz savoy cabbage
- 2 teaspoons of pureed garlic
- 1 teaspoon of parsley
- 1 tablespoon of fresh thyme
- Handful of fresh spinach
- Salt and pepper to season
- 100g / 3.5oz broccoli
- 4 spears of asparagus
- Vegetable cube of oxo
- 1 teaspoon of Greek yoghurt
- 1 tablespoon of fresh mint
- Handful of frozen peas
- 200ml / 6.76oz water

Instructions:

1. Clean the vegetables

2. Chop the asparagus into slices of approx. 1cm, chop the broccoli into florets, slice the fresh herbs, cabbage, and spinach

3. Put all the vegetables into the bottom of the soup maker

4. Add 200ml of water on top of the vegetables

5. Add all seasonings including the oxo cube

6. Cook for 28 minutes

7. Once cooked add the garlic and stir the soup thoroughly, and blend

8. Serve immediately with a teaspoon of Greek yoghurt on the top

Separated Salad Soup

Time: 30 minutes / Serving 4
Net Carbs: 16g / 0.56oz Fat: 0g / 0.00oz
Protein: 2g / 0.07oz. Kcal: 75

Ingredients:

- ¼ of white cabbage
- 1 red pepper
- 3 sticks of celery
- 1 teaspoon of oregano
- Salt and pepper
- 1 green pepper
- 4 carrots
- 2 tomatoes
- 100ml / 3.4oz water

Instructions:

1. Deseed the peppers, peel the carrots and then chop all salad items
2. Add all ingredients to your soup maker
3. Cook for 25 minutes on the blend feature
4. Serve

28 Day Meal Plan

Day One

Breakfast – Mango Marvellous Lassi

Time: 10 minutes / Serving 6

Net Carbs: 20g / 0.70oz Fat: 3g / 0.10oz

Protein: 5g / 0.18oz Kcal: 131

Ingredients:

- 3 -4 ripe honey mangoes
- 500g / 17.6oz natural yoghurt
- Juice from 2 limes
- 1 tablespoon of honey
- Pinch of cardamon

Instructions:

1. Add everything apart from the lime juice to your soup maker and blend until smooth
2. Add the lime juice a bit at a time
3. Keep trying the drink until it is the right consistency and flavour for you
4. Pour over ice cubes and enjoy

Lunch – Colourful Coriander & Carrot Soup (See page 32)

Dinner – Cheeky Chicken Soup (See page 54)

Day Two

Breakfast – Berry Mixed Smoothie (See page 18)

Lunch – Marvellous Mushroom Soup (See page 31)

Dinner – Lively Leftover Soup

Time: 30 minutes / Serving 4

Net Carbs: 21g / 0.74oz Fat: 0g / 0.00oz

Protein: 5g / 0.18oz Kcal: 104

Ingredients:

- ½ courgette
- 5 peeled carrots
- ½ small cauliflower
- 468ml / 15.8oz water
- 1 small broccoli
- 1 medium leek
- 1 teaspoon of parsley
- Salt and pepper

Instructions:

1. Chop the vegetables and add to your soup maker

2. Add the seasoning and water

3. Mix thoroughly

4. Choose the cook and blend feature and cook for 25 – 30 minutes

5. Serve and enjoy

Breakfast – Two Minute Breakfast Shake (See page 21)

Lunch – Clever Celery Soup

Time: 30 minutes / Serving 4

Net Carbs: 10g / 0.35oz Fat: 3g / 0.10oz

Protein: 2g / 0.07oz Kcal: 76

Ingredients:

- 6 sticks of celery
- 1 large onion
- 4 large carrots, peeled
- 250ml / 8.5oz water

- 2 tablespoons soft cheese
- 1 teaspoon chives
- 1 teaspoon mixed herbs
- Salt and pepper

Instructions:

1. Chop the celery and add to your soup maker
2. Dice the carrots and onions and add to the soup maker
3. Add the water and seasoning and use the cook and blend function for 30 minutes
4. Add the soft cheese and blend
5. Serve and enjoy

Dinner – Tasty Turkey Soup (See page 51)

Day Four

Breakfast – Terrific Tropical Smooth Bowl
Time: 20 minutes / Serving 2
Net Carbs: 41g / 1.45oz Fat: 15g / 0.53oz
Protein: 4g / 0.14oz Kcal: 332

Ingredients:

- 1 stoned, peeled, and chunked ripe mango
- 200g / 7.1oz cored, peeled, and chunked pineapple
- 2 halved passion fruits deseeded
- 2 ripe bananas
- Handful of blueberries
- 2 tablespoons coconut yoghurt
- 150ml / 5fl oz of coconut milk
- 2 tablespoons flaked coconut
- Mint leaves

Instructions:

1. Add the pineapple, bananas, mango, coconut milk and yoghurt into your soup maker and pulse until smooth and thick
2. Pour into two bowls and decorate with the fruits, flakes, and mint leaves

Lunch – Tasty Tomato Soup (See page 33)

Dinner – Cheddar Potato & Sausage Soup (See page 57)

Breakfast – Super Breakfast Shake (See page 20)

Lunch – Fancy French and Onion Soup

Time: 30 minutes / Serving 4
Net Carbs: 19g / 0.67oz Fat: 0g / 0.00oz
Protein: 3g / 0.10oz Kcal: 94

Ingredients:

- ◉ 250ml / 8.5oz of water
- ◉ 5 peeled onions
- ◉ 3 peeled carrots
- ◉ 5 sticks of celery
- ◉ 2 tablespoons Greek yoghurt
- ◉ 2 teaspoons of chives
- ◉ 1 teaspoon of thyme
- ◉ 1 teaspoon of mixed herbs
- ◉ Salt and pepper

Instructions:

1. Dice the onion, celery and carrots and add to your soup maker
2. Add the water and seasoning
3. Add the Greek yoghurt
4. Cook using the chunky soup program for 30 minutes
5. Enjoy

Dinner – Perfect Pea and Ham Soup (See page 56)

Day Six

Breakfast – Beautiful Banana Smoothie (See page 22)

Lunch – Lentil Soup (See page 29)

Dinner – Lemon Greek Chicken

Time: 40 minutes / Serving 4
Net Carbs: 41g / 1.45oz Fat: 0g / 0.00oz
Protein: 10g / 0.35oz Kcal: 217

Ingredients:

- 1 boneless and skinless chicken breast
- 1 large onion
- 1 red pepper
- 2 tablespoons/1/8 of a cup of garlic puree
- 2 teaspoons of chives
- 150ml / 5fl oz of water
- 3 tablespoons of Greek yoghurt
- Salt and pepper
- 1 large juice & zest of a lemon
- 1 cup of couscous
- ½ cup of feta cheese

Instructions:

1. Peel and dice the onion, dice the pepper, and dice the chicken breast and put into the soup maker

2. Add the lemon, water, couscous, and seasoning

3. Cook for 25 minutes on the chunky soup program

4. Add the feta cheese and yoghurt and blend

5. Serve and enjoy

Day Seven

Breakfast – Quick Kiwi Smoothie

Time: 5 minutes / Serving 2-3
Net Carbs: 36g / 1.27oz Fat: 1g / 0.03oz
Protein: 2g / 0.07oz Kcal: 163

Ingredients:

- 3 peeled kiwi fruit
- 1 peeled, stoned and chopped mango
- 1 sliced banana
- 500ml / 16.9oz pineapple juice

Instructions:

1. Place everything into your soup maker and blend until smooth
2. Transfer to 2-3 tall glasses and enjoy

Lunch – Banging Butternut Squash Soup (See page 34)

Dinner – Sensational Stilton & Broccoli Soup (See page 53)

Day Eight

Breakfast – Super Strawberry & Green Smoothie (See page 23)

Lunch – Soup Maker Chicken Noodle Soup

Time: 30 minutes / Serving 4

Net Carbs: 34g / 1.20oz Fat: 6g / 0.21oz

Protein: 8g / 0.28oz Kcal: 230

Ingredients:

- 1 chicken breast
- 150g / 2/3 of a cup of linguine pasta
- 1 carrot
- 1 onion
- 2 teaspoons of garlic puree
- 2 teaspoons of oregano
- 1 teaspoon of basil
- 2 teaspoons of tarragon
- 1 teaspoon thyme
- 2 teaspoons of paprika
- 2 tablespoons butter
- 100ml / 3.4oz of water
- Salt and pepper

Instructions:

1. Chop the chicken into bite size pieces

2. Peel and dice the carrot and onion

3. Put the chicken, pasta, vegetables, and seasoning into your soup maker

4. Add the water and cook on the chunky soup function for 25 minutes

5. Add the butter and mix thoroughly

Dinner – Roast Dinner Soup (See page 50)

Day Nine

Breakfast – Gorgeous Green Smoothie
Time: 5 minutes / Serving 1
Net Carbs: 36g / 1.27oz Fat: 15g / 0.53oz
Protein: 8g / 0.28oz Kcal: 329

Ingredients:

- 250ml / 8.5oz milk
- 1 tablespoon of ground flaxseed
- 1 small ripe banana
- 1 stoned medjool date
- Handful of spinach
- 1 tablespoon of almond butter
- Pinch of cinnamon

Instructions:

1. Place everything into your soup maker and blend until smooth
2. Pour in a glass and enjoy

Lunch – 50 Calorie Green Goodness Soup (See page 30)

Dinner – Minestrone Homemade Soup (See page 52)

Day Ten

Breakfast – Remarkable Raspberry & Awesome Apple Smoothie (See page 24)

Lunch – Basic Broccoli Soup

Time: 30 minutes / Serving 3
Net Carbs: 11g / 0.39oz Fat: 3g / 0.10oz
Protein: 5g / 0.18oz Kcal: 162

Ingredients:

- 500ml / 16.9oz vegetable stock
- 300ml / 10.1oz semi skimmed milk
- ½ teaspoon sea salt
- 1 tablespoon of cornflour with 2 tablespoons of water
- 300g / 10.6oz broccoli
- 1 small onion
- Pinch of black pepper

Instructions:

1. Cut the broccoli into small florets
2. Diced the onion
3. Add all the ingredients to your soup maker
4. Set the soup maker to the smooth setting
5. Cook for 10–15 minutes then pulse and serve

Dinner – Magnificent Mac n Cheese (See page 60)

Breakfast – Cheerful Cherry Smoothie (See page 27)

Lunch – Luscious Leek & Potato Soup (See page 35)

Dinner – Soup Maker Veggie Bowls of Pasta

Time: 30 minutes / Serving 4

Net Carbs: 45g / 1.59oz Fat: 1g / 0.03oz

Protein: 8g / 0.28oz Kcal: 267

Ingredients:

- 50g / 1/3 of a cup of green beans
- 50g / 1/3 of a cup of tin of kidney beans
- 150g / 2/3 of a cup of pasta shapes
- 1 onion
- 1 carrot
- 1 potato
- ½ a courgette
- 1 tin of tomatoes
- 1/3 glass of red wine
- 2 teaspoons of garlic puree
- 2 teaspoons of oregano
- 1 teaspoon of basil
- 1 teaspoon of thyme
- 2 teaspoons of paprika
- Salt and pepper

Instructions:

1. Dice the green beans

2. Peel and dice the carrot, potato, and onion

3. Slice the courgette

4. Put the vegetables, beans, pasta, and seasoning into the soup maker

5. Add the tinned tomatoes and red well, mix to combine

6. Select the chunky soup setting and cook for 25 minutes

Day Twelve

Breakfast – Tasty Turmeric Smooth Bowl
Time: 10 minutes / Serving 2
Net Carbs: 40g / 1.41oz Fat: 10g / 0.35oz
Protein: 7g / 0.25oz Kcal: 291

Ingredients:

- 3 tablespoons of coconut milk
- 2 teaspoon ground turmeric
- 50g / 1/3 of a cup of oats
- Handful of cashew nuts
- 2 peeled and chopped bananas
- ½ tablespoon of ground cinnamon
- 1 tablespoon chopped nuts
- 600ml / 20.2oz of water

Instructions:

1. Add everything to your soup maker except the chopped nuts and blend until smooth

2. Serve topped with the chopped nuts

Lunch – Soup Maker Portuguese Fish Soup (See page 36)

Dinner – Tasty Turkey Soup (See page 51)

Day Thirteen

Breakfast – Curly Kale Smoothie (See page 26)

Lunch – Vegetable Thai Soup Maker Curry (See page 40)

Dinner – Perfect Prawn Indian Soup

Time: 30 minutes / Serving 4
Net Carbs: 34g / 1.20oz Fat: 6g / 0.21oz
Protein: 8g / 0.28oz Kcal: 230

Ingredients:

- 2000g / 70.5oz of fresh prawns
- 1 onion
- 1 teaspoon of mixed spice
- 1 teaspoon of paprika
- 1 teaspoon of garlic puree
- 4 tablespoons Greek yoghurt
- Salt and pepper
- 1 red pepper
- 3 teaspoons of coriander
- 4 teaspoons of curry powder
- 2 teaspoons of ginger puree
- 1 juice and rind from a lime
- 100ml / 3.4oz fish stock

Instructions:

1. Peel and dice the onion, dice the pepper, and put them both into the soup maker with the prawns with shells removed

2. Add the fish stock and spices

3. Cook on the blend feature for 25 minutes

4. Once cooked add the lime and Greek yoghurt and blend

5. Serve and enjoy

Day Fourteen

Breakfast – Cheerful Cherry Smoothie (See page 27)

Lunch – Majestic Mediterranean Veggie Soup (See page 37)

Dinner – Herb & Vegetable Soup

Time: 30 minutes / Serving 2

Net Carbs: 32g / 1.13oz Fat: 1g / 0.03oz

Protein: 4g / 0.14oz. Kcal: 166

Ingredients:

- 200g / 7.1oz chopped vegetables of your choice
- 300g / 10.6oz peeled and chopped potatoes
- 700ml / 23.7oz of vegetable stock
- Fresh herbs and crème fraiche to serve

Instructions:

1. Add all ingredients to your soup maker
2. Cook for 25 minutes using the smooth soup function
3. Pour into bowls, add a spoonful of crème fraiche and sprinkle with fresh herbs

Day Fifteen

Lunch – Blended Broccoli Soup (See page 44)

Dinner – Separated Salad Soup (See page 66)

Dessert – Sensational Smooth Jellies with Ice Cream

Time: 1 hour 5 minutes / Serving 12

Net Carbs: 15g / 0.53oz Fat: 2g / 0.07oz

Protein: 4g / 0.14oz Kcal: 92

Ingredients:

- 🍽 1000ml / 33.8oz mango, orange, and passion fruit smoothie

- 🍽 6 sheets of leaf gelatine

- 🍽 500ml / 16.9oz tub of vanilla ice cream

Instructions:

1. Add the leaf gelatine to a bowl of cold water and cover

2. Leave the gelatine until soft (about 4 minutes)

3. Put the smoothie liquid into the soup maker and heat

4. Turn the soup maker off

5. Take the gelatine from the water

6. Add the gelatine to the soup maker

7. Blend and stir well

8. Pour into 12 glasses

9. Put in the fridge for at least 1 hour to set

10. Serve with a small scoop of vanilla ice cream

Day Sixteen

Lunch – Complete Cauliflower Soup (See page 48)

Dinner – Ravishing Rainbow Bowl (See page 59)

Dessert – Cubie Smoothie

Time: 5 minutes / Serving 12

Net Carbs: 0g / 0.00oz Fat: 0g / 0.00oz

Protein: 0g / 0.00oz Kcal: 0

Ingredients:

- Strawberries
- Raspberries
- Blackberries
- Mango
- Passion fruit

Instructions:

1. Add the fruits to your soup maker and pulse until a puree consistency
2. Sieve to remove pips
3. Pour into ice trays
4. Freeze

When ready remove from ice tray, add a banana, yoghurt, and honey to create a superb dish

Day Seventeen

Lunch – Noodle Soup with Chicken

Time: 30 minutes / Serving 4
Net Carbs: 34g / 1.20oz Fat: 6g / 0.21oz
Protein: 8g / 0.28oz. Kcal: 230

Ingredients:

- 1 chicken breast
- 150g / 2/3 of a cup of pasta linguine
- 1 carrot
- 1 onion
- 2 teaspoons of oregano
- 2 teaspoons of tarragon
- 1 teaspoon of basil
- 1 teaspoon of thyme
- 2 teaspoons of garlic puree
- 2 teaspoons of paprika
- 2 tablespoons butter
- 100ml / 3.38oz water
- Salt and pepper

Instructions:

1. Dice the chicken into small pieces

2. Peel and dice the carrots and onion

3. Place the chicken, vegetables, seasoning and pasta into the soup maker

4. Add the water and cook on the chunky soup function for 25 minutes

5. Once cooked add the butter and mix thoroughly

6. Serve

Dinner – Pea Minty Soup (See page 61)

Lunch – Roast Chicken Soup

Time: 35 minutes / Serving 2
Net Carbs: 8g / 0.28oz Fat: 5g / 0.18oz
Protein: 17g / 0.60oz Kcal: 155

Ingredients:

- 1 onion, chopped
- ½ teaspoon thyme
- 1 large carrot, chopped
- 700ml / 23.7oz chicken stock
- 150g / 5.3oz roast chicken, shredded
- 100g / 3.5oz frozen peas
- ½ garlic clove, crushed
- 1 ½ tablespoon Greek yoghurt
- Lemon juice

Instructions:

1. Put the onion, carrots, stock, thyme, and peas into the soup maker

2. Select the 'chunky soup' function – make sure you do not fill the soup maker too much

3. Once the cycle is complete, stir in the shredded roast chicken

4. Leave the mix to warm through

5. Mix yoghurt, garlic, and lemon juice in a small bowl

6. Season soup and pour into bowls; garnish with yoghurt and serve

Dinner – Moroccan Creamy Carrot Soup (See page 62)

Lunch – Potato Sweet Soup (See page 45)

Dinner – Spiced Carrot and Lentil Soup

Time: 25 minutes / Serving 4
Net Carbs: 34g / 1.20oz Fat: 7g / 0.25oz
Protein: 11g / 0.39oz Kcal: 238

Ingredients:

- 2 teaspoons cumin seeds
- Pinch of chilli flakes
- 2 tablespoons olive oil
- 600g / 21.2oz carrots, washed and grated
- 140g / 4.9oz split red lentils
- 1000ml / 33.8oz vegetable stock
- 125ml / 4.2oz milk
- Plain yoghurt and naan bread to serve

Instructions:

1. In a large saucepan, heat, and dry fry the cumin seeds and chilli flakes for approximately 1 minute

2. Put aside half; to the pan, add oil, carrots, split red lentils, vegetable stock and milk and bring to the boil

3. Simmer for 15 minutes, or until the lentils are softened and swollen

4. Blend mixture or leave chunky if you prefer

5. Season to taste

6. Serve with a large spoonful of yoghurt, sprinkle of spices (the reserves from earlier) and warmed naan breads

Day Twenty

Lunch – Utterly, Buttery Butternut Squash Soup (See page 46)

Dinner – Colourful Carrot and Coriander Soup

Time: 35 minutes / Serving 2

Net Carbs: 17g / 0.60oz Fat: 2g / 0.07oz

Protein: 9g / 0.32oz. Kcal: 133

Ingredients:

- 1 small onion, chopped
- 1 small potato, peeled and chopped
- ½ teaspoon ground coriander
- 600ml / 20.3oz vegetable stock (can use chicken stock if preferred)
- 400g / 14.1oz carrots, peeled and diced
- ½ bunch of coriander

Instructions:

1. Add all ingredients into the soup maker, minus the coriander
2. Select the 'smooth soup' function
3. Once complete, season the soup and add the coriander
4. Blend once again until the coriander is mixed well
5. Serve

Day Twenty-One

Lunch – Vegetable Thai Soup Maker Curry (See page 40)

Dinner – Creamy Carrot and Swede Soup

Time: 35 minutes / Serving 4

Net Carbs: 24g / 0.85oz Fat: 0g / 0.00oz

Protein: 2g / 0.07oz. Kcal: 108

Ingredients:

- 10 carrots
- 1 teaspoon of pureed garlic
- 3 tablespoons of sage
- Salt and pepper
- 1 swede
- 1 vegetable oxo cube
- 2 tablespoons of parsley
- 1600ml / 54.1oz of water

Instructions:

1. Peel the swede and carrots and dice into small cubes

2. Put 1600ml of water into the bottom of the soup maker then add the carrot and swede

3. Cook using the chunky soup setting for 28 minutes

4. Once cooked you will have plenty of liquid therefore remove 400ml of stock to use another day

5. Mix everything well so that it is covered with liquid but not drowning

6. Season, blend and serve

Lunch – Bonfire Pumpkin Soup

Time: 30 minutes / Serving 2
Net Carbs: 7g / 0.25oz Fat: 1g / 0.03oz
Protein: 1g / 0.03oz Kcal: 39

Ingredients:

- 500g / 17.6oz of pumpkin cubes
- 1 onion
- Salt and pepper
- 3 cloves of garlic
- 2 teaspoons of mixed herbs
- 200ml / 6.8oz of water

Instructions:

1. Peel and slice the onion and garlic and put into the soup maker with the cubed pumpkin
2. Season with the mixed herbs, salt, and pepper
3. Add 200ml of water
4. Set the soup maker to cook on the chunky soup setting
5. Once the soup is cooked check to see that there is enough liquid to blend into a smooth soup
6. Pour into bowls and serve

Dinner – Cheesy Cauliflower Soup (See page 63)

Day Twenty-Three

Lunch – Parsnip Perfection Soup (See page 41)

Dinner – Crab and Cream of Cauliflower Soup

Time: 30 minutes / Serving 4
Net Carbs: 10g / 0.35oz Fat: 22g / 0.78oz
Protein: 10g / 0.35oz Kcal: 411

Ingredients:

- 1 cauliflower
- 1 glass of white dry wine
- 50g / 1.8oz cheddar cheese
- 2 teaspoons of parsley
- 100ml / 3.38oz fish stock
- Fresh chives
- 1 large crab with the meat removed
- 8 bacon rashers
- 2 teaspoons of mustard
- 2 teaspoons of pureed garlic
- 1 juice and rind of a lemon
- Salt and pepper to season

Instructions:

1. Cut the cauliflower into small florets

2. Put the crab meat, cauliflower florets, 7 rashers of bacon, 25g of the cheddar cheese and the season (except the chives) into your soup maker

3. Add the wine, fish stock, and cook for 25 minutes on the blend soup function

4. Once cooked add the lemon and mix thoroughly

5. Divide into bowls, add the remainder of the cheese

6. Decorate with the remaining bacon and top with the fresh chives

Day Twenty-Four

Lunch – Clearly Skinny Celery Soup (See page 43)

Dinner – Broccoli Gratin Soup

Time: 35 minutes / Serving 4
Net Carbs: 16g / 0.56oz Fat: 9g / 0.32oz
Protein: 8g / 0.28oz. Kcal: 169

Ingredients:

- 2 large carrots
- 75g / 2.6oz courgette
- ¼ of a large cauliflower
- 50g / 1.8oz cheese
- 2 teaspoons of parsley
- 100ml / 3.4oz water
- 1 small head of broccoli
- ½ an onion
- 1 teaspoon of garlic puree
- 1 tablespoon of soft cheese
- 4 tablespoons of coconut milk
- Salt and pepper

Instructions:

1. Slice and dice the carrots and onion

2. Cut the courgette, cauliflower, and broccoli into chunks

3. Add all the vegetables to your soup maker and cook for 25 minutes

4. Once the vegetables are cooked drain the liquid off

5. Add the cheese, coconut milk, parsley, garlic and salt and pepper to the vegetables in the soup maker

6. Blend

7. Serve and enjoy

Day Twenty-Five

Lunch – Cauliflower Squashed Soup

Time: 30 minutes / Serving 6
Net Carbs: 19g / 0.67oz Fat: 0g / 0.00oz
Protein: 3g / 0.10oz. Kcal: 85

Ingredients:

- 1 medium cauliflower
- 1 peeled and seedless butternut squash
- 4 tablespoons of Greek yoghurt
- 1 teaspoon of parsley
- Salt and pepper
- 1 peeled large onion
- 1 yellow pepper
- 250ml / 8.5oz water
- 1 teaspoon of mixed herbs

Instructions:

1. Chop the cauliflower into small florets and add to your soup maker
2. Chop the pepper and remove the seeds then add to your soup maker
3. Chop the butternut squash and onions and add to soup maker
4. Add the water and season

Dinner – Moroccan Creamy Carrot Soup (See page 62)

Lunch – Broccoli Gratin Soup

Time: 35 minutes / Serving 4
Net Carbs: 16g / 0.56oz Fat: 9g / 0.32oz
Protein: 8g / 0.28oz. Kcal: 169

Ingredients:

- 2 large carrots
- 75g / 2.7oz courgette
- ¼ of a large cauliflower
- 50g / 1.8oz cheese
- 2 teaspoons of parsley
- 100ml / 3.4oz water
- 1 small head of broccoli
- ½ an onion
- 1 teaspoon of garlic puree
- 1 tablespoon of soft cheese
- 4 tablespoons of coconut milk
- Salt and pepper

Instructions:

1. Slice and dice the carrots and onion

2. Cut the courgette, cauliflower, and broccoli into chunks

3. Add all the vegetables to your soup maker and cook for 25 minutes

4. Once the vegetables are cooked drain the liquid off

5. Add the cheese, coconut milk, parsley, garlic and salt and pepper to the vegetables in the soup maker

6. Blend

7. Serve and enjoy

Dinner – Herb & Vegetable Soup (See page 86)

Lunch – Bolognese Pasta Soup

Time: 33 minutes / Serving 4
Net Carbs: 30g / 1.06oz Fat: 11g / 0.39oz
Protein: 8g / 0.28oz. Kcal: 108

Ingredients:

- 1 tablespoon olive oil
- 2 garlic cloves, chopped
- 1 onion, chopped
- 1 red pepper, diced
- 180g / 6.4oz dried pasta

- 500g / 17.6oz passata
- 700ml / 23.7oz beef stock
- 1 teaspoon oregano
- 250g / 8.8oz mined beef, cooked

Instructions:

1. Optional step: fry the onions, garlic and pepper in oil
2. Add all the ingredients to the soup maker and mix together
3. Set the soup maker to 'chunky soup'
4. Season if required and serve

Dinner – Greek Greens Soup (See page 64)

Day Twenty-Eight

Lunch – Cocktail of Prawn Soup (See page 47)

Dinner – Russian Wild Mushroom and Barley Soup

Time: 60 minutes / Serving 4-6
Net Carbs: 31g / 1.09oz Fat: 7g / 0.25oz
Protein: 8g / 0.28oz Kcal: 217

Ingredients:

- 30g / 1.1oz dried porcini mushrooms
- 20g / 0.7oz unsalted butter
- 1 ½ tablespoons olive oil
- 250g / 8.8oz mushrooms, chopped
- 1 carrot, peeled and diced
- 1 celery stick, diced
- 200g / 7.1oz pearl barley
- 800ml / 27.1oz chicken or beef stock
- Dill, leaves chopped
- Soured cream and bread to serve

Instructions:

1. Pour 750ml of boiling water onto the porcini mushrooms and allow to soak

2. Heat butter and olive oil in a saucepan and add the mushrooms, celery and carrots

3. Fry mix over a medium-high heat for 10 minutes, until the carrots are turning a dark gold

4. To the mix, add barley and stir for 2 minutes

5. Pour in the stock

6. Drain the porcini and keep the liquid

7. Pour both the liquor and porcini into the pan

8. Turn down the heat and simmer for 30 minutes, or until barley is tender

9. Stir in the dill and season to taste

10. Serve with a spoonful of soured cream and crusty bread

Printed in Great Britain
by Amazon